To & Ron

From Bill
▽
Sue

Prophecies of Love

KAHLIL GIBRAN

PROPHECIES OF LOVE

Reflections From the Heart

Selected by Julie Clardy

Illustrated by Ginnie Scott

♛ Hallmark Editions

PROPHECIES OF LOVE

Life without love is like a
tree without blossom and
fruit. And love without
beauty is like flowers
without scent
and fruits
without seeds.

For love, all of existence is
an eternal shrine.

Love is a precious treasure,
   it is God's gift to sensitive
   and great spirits.

The first glance
from the eyes of the beloved
is like the spirit
that moved
upon the face of the waters,
giving birth
to heaven
and earth.

...Love...
It surrounds every being
and extends slowly
to embrace
all that shall be.

Joining of lips
in love
reveals heavenly secrets
which the tongue
cannot utter!

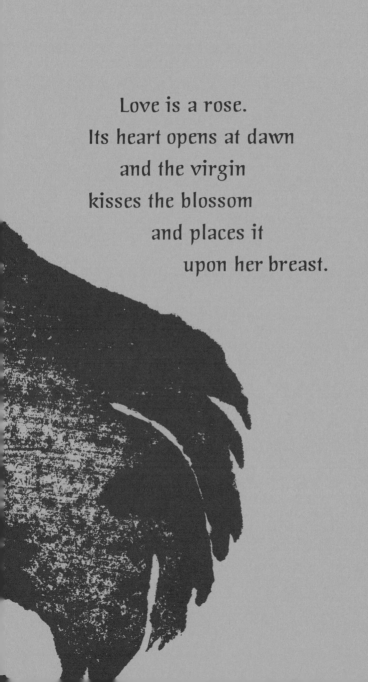

Love is a rose.
Its heart opens at dawn
and the virgin
kisses the blossom
and places it
upon her breast.

Had it not been for seeing
    and hearing,
light and sound would have been
        naught but confusion
        and pulsations in space.
Likewise,
    had it not been
        for the heart you love,
you would have been a fine dust
    blown and scattered
        by the wind.

Love prides itself
not only
    in the one who loves,
but also
    in the beloved.

Real beauty
lies in the spiritual accord
that is called love
which can exist between
a man
and a woman.

Love
is the only flower
　　that grows
　　　　and blossoms
without the aid
　　of seasons.

Life is divided
into two halves,
one frozen, the other aflame;

the burning half is love.

Love and emptiness
in us
are like the sea's ebb
and flow.

Limited love
        asks for possession
    of the beloved,
but the unlimited
    asks only
        for itself.

Love is the gentle smile
upon the lips
of beauty.

How savage is love
    that plants a flower
    and uproots a field;
that revives us
    for a day
        and stuns us
            for an age!

Love is a magic ray
emitted from the burning core
of the soul
and illuminating
the surrounding earth.

It enables us
    to perceive life
    as a beautiful dream
between one awakening
    and another.

All can hear,
   but only the sensitive
      can understand....

Love is the only freedom
in the world
because it so elevates the spirit
that the laws of humanity
and the phenomena
of nature
do not alter its course.

Gifts alone
do not entice love;
parting does not discourage love;
poverty does not chase love;
jealousy does not prove its
awareness;
madness does not evidence its
presence.

Love

is a trembling

happiness.

Set in York, a calligraphic roman face
designed for the Visual Graphics Corporation.
Typography by Hallmark Photo Composition.
Printed in specially selected match colors
on Gold Sonata Vellum by Hopper.
Designed by Jay D. Johnson.